love can be red

Poems by: Amanda Ace

To those who have been burned by love.

To those who have begged for love.

Remember love can be red but it is not supposed to hurt.

content warning: a few poems contain blood
and violence

My intense longing
to feel love
has me begging
and pleading
with a door
that's already been shut
in my face.

The burning desire
has brought me
to my knees
a mess
on your doorstep
scrounging for crumbs
and smiling
on an empty stomach.

I wanna write a poem

about the way you make love to me

and then I wanna write a poem

about how it's not love at all

a poem that's fast and empty

but sounds good when you read it for the first time

before you face the longing it'll bring

it will be pretty with its words

but lack a deeper meaning

you'll feel it everywhere

yet nowhere at all

you're a poem

that makes me moan and ache

a poem that I keep adding lines to

even after I've ran out of ink

I've touched you everywhere

yet nowhere at all.

I'd burn myself

to the ground

if I knew a spark

would reach your feet.

I refuse

to let you forget

about me

even if I have to burn myself

to the ground

you will choke

on the smoke you created.

I pray

your kisses

leave a mark

so when the light

surrounds me

others can see

the way you love me

in the dark.

I'm on the bathroom floor
begging for your love
while you're in between
her legs
forgetting you once knew
my name
waiting for a text
I grab onto the sink
and imagine the way she arches
her back
fingers in hair
that I cut
she's oblivious
to the fact
that a night
she may forget
is now tattooed
across my skin
I will have to think about this for centuries
longer than those present
the sex I wasn't apart of
is a memory
I'll never escape
no matter how many times
I wipe my skin clean.

-I shouldn't have to live with your mistakes

Your kisses

bring dermatographia

and I'm left

feeling your lips

for centuries

though their presence

was merely seconds

I have gentle skin

and you have rough hands

-when will you learn this?

I told you

I was done

begging

for you

but my knees

are bruised

and the silence

is bleeding

through my chest.

I can't escape your touch
though I haven't felt it in months.

No matter how hard
my friends pull me
and plead
I'm rooted to the ground
outside your front door
staring at this wall
you built
just to slam
in my face
I swear the light
on the welcome sign
still flickers
though I watched you
cut the cord.

One day I'll love myself
enough
to move on
but today
I'm rooted to the ground
outside your front door

I wish you'd never let me in.

My sheets no longer reek

of your lies

my pillows erased the stretch

of your betrayal

my comforter battled

your empty promises

until a bloody victor

but I still wake up

on your side of the bed.

The blood has been cleaned

from the street

my wounds

have been sewn shut

but every so often

I still see traces of red.

You're the cigarette

I can't put down

even after my lungs

have gone black

The thought of you

makes me sick

to my stomach

yet I can't stop reaching

for you.

Grabbing my lighter

I know I'll regret you

in the morning

when I wake up

coughing

but I'll let this one

burn slowly.

I bled

for your love

and I'm left

without a scar

as proof

because the love

was never deep enough

for stitches.

I teach in a classroom

where my voice is tuned out

and talked over.

I tread on begging

for respect and compliance

only to be met with more noise

to requests I never sought out.

I teach in a classroom

where you sit front row

yet remain absent.

My lessons have been carefully crafted for you

yet you'd rather laugh with your peers

so I grow silent and wait.

I teach in a classroom

where I shut off the lights after school

and pray tomorrow you'll be different.

You,

didn't exist
I painted all the lines darker
and was met with a blank canvas
Like an artist
I'm used to arranging the colors
how I want them to be
but I cannot paint you
the same way
I bring a canvas to life.
To make you love me
would be adding pigment
to a color that
doesn't exist.

Lipstick

permanently

tainting

his lips

Perfume

filling the air

I used to breathe

Handprints

forever

plastered

across his chest.

Will I ever be able to kiss him without tasting her?

To take someone back

There are days

where I question

why I ever stayed gone

and

there are days

where I can't touch you

without reaching her

and

running to the bathroom

so you don't see the acid

escape my lips.

As I wipe my mouth and let my hair back down

I can't even look in the mirror as

I cower back into the room

where I'll let you do it all over again

-the things I do for love.

The least you could have done

was stop the bleeding

but you'd never turn away

from red

so you watch as it glistens

while the color slips away

from my face

I don't want

to have to lie here

on the street

bleeding out

for you

but if that's what you need

then pass me

the blade.

-loving you is like

I can't fall asleep
so I picture a world
in which you want
to spend time with me

I'm tossing and turning
it's 5 am
you want me in the same way I want you
we're in the bedroom
and you're teaching me how to play guitar
by the time I wake up
I still won't know how to play a single instrument

I can't fall asleep
so my eyelids
become your face.

I'm rolling around in a bed
where you love me back
I'll fall asleep
once I'm yours
or I'll lie awake trying.

I only ever write good poetry

when I'm in pain.

So, I text that boy

I love him

knowing he doesn't feel the same

and I leave a love letter at his door

knowing he won't return one back

I only ever write good poetry

when I'm in pain.

Will art always make me bleed?

I miss you

from your barren lips

is a slap to the face

compliments aren't supposed to hurt

yet I cry and wince

when you tell me you love me

and I brace myself for impact.

I was bleeding

and finally

it wasn't for you

but

unfortunately

all blood is red.

Seeing him now

feels like a knife poking her stomach

rather than stabbing

its way through her heart

one day

the knife won't reach

her at all

but

only she can remove it

from her own hands.

Your promise

is a threat

invading the barriers

of my soul

I beg for retreat

yet you only repeat

I miss you

while staying on your side

of the bed.

Your promise is a threat

so you make sure it's never loud enough

I think you like it that way.

I like the way scars look

across my skin

so I let you

hold me.

With false encouragement
and your phone in my hand
I scroll for answers
until I find a truth
I'm not ready to taste
I will never look like this myth
they're forcing
down our throats
why were men gifted eyes
just to wonder
a woman is a painting
to be adored
not compared
to mechanically crafted
museums of lies
Da Vinci
didn't paint the Mona Lisa
to look away
and spend his days staring
at portraits that don't exist

Cherish the real person in front of you.

Comparing my body

to bodies that don't exist

Aching for likes

from boys

whose best version

doesn't exist

Seeking out

to find that same happiness

that offline

doesn't exist

Wishing you could be somebody else

who beyond filters

doesn't exist.

-social media

In your arms I shrink

back into myself

until there's nothing left

but bones

to hold on to

with every kiss

I start to love you more

and me less.

I shouldn't have to bleed

for you to notice me

but my actions battle my mind daily

and inflict pain throughout my being

love is not supposed to hurt

I shouldn't have to beg

for you to listen

but you stay in the other room

so I shout across the distance

bouncing off walls to someone indifferent

love is not supposed to hurt.

I deleted

your number

but not before saving it

in my notes app

I'm always one foot in

doors I should lock

and lingering

in hallways

I should have never entered.

The new girl

In case no one has told you

nothing good

comes from looking

at the new opponent

the new one

treated with malice

and cruelty

the new one

subject to your callous mistakes

with a player like that

you're never really the teammate

she must like to bleed

and if not she will learn

to stitch up her own wounds.

I love you

shouldn't hurt

but it's written on a knife

that you slid into my chest

3 words

followed by 6 acts

proving you don't

your words mutilate

when they're stripped clean

from my hands and tarnished

like they came

I love you

shouldn't scar

but every confession is a bullet

I can't learn to dodge.

I want to fall asleep in a bed

where you love me back

but I can't seem to find that place

I told myself if I thought about you enough

you'd feel it like a slap to the face

funny how I'm the only one in pain.

A ghost

is someone you've had to miss

more than you ever got to hold.

You're the first line

to every poem

I write

and it doesn't matter

what words I add

to the space in between

because it always ends

with you

not loving me back.

In college

I was taught

we all have our own associations

that are just ours

and no one else's.

These associations can relate to a certain person

or place in time.

They can stem from a tree branch

opera music

or a man walking down the street.

That day I left class

hopeful

-maybe you do still think about me.

Love shouldn't bring pain

I know this

but I burn

when I feel

and I sob

when I desire

I bleed

when I yearn

and I wince

when I chase

love shouldn't bring pain

I know this

but I know myself

and romantic love

has only ever hurt.

I am not a fool

for you

I am a fool

for love

but unfortunately

those two statements

look the same.

You're unattainable

and I'm not used to failing

so I reach

for a concept

I don't have hands for.

I want a love

that doesn't make me bleed,

feelings

that don't make me weep,

I want to reach out to you

without feeling like I'm begging

and pleading,

I don't want it to be easy,

I don't want it to always hurt,

I want the rush

without the fall

that comes with it

I guess I just want to feel like I can love you

without it making me sad.

The difference

between

love

and

in love

is

you

and

me.

How can I love you

and hate you?

The answers stuck

between the treatment

and the attachment

The fool hoping

one will change.

I've held

every boy

who's wronged me

close in my arms

time and time again

after betrayal

what used to feel like home

now shattered

with remembrance

and the question of what I'm doing here.

I lie

on the bathroom floor

and

convince myself

having half of you

is better than

not having you at all.

Loving you

is playing hide and go seek

but you're not coming to find me,

playing tag

but I'm the only fool running.

Why play the games

if they're this way and

why love someone

in the same unfavorable manner?

Seek someone

who always finds you

and chase someone

who follows you

at the same speed.

Someone worth

dying for

would never kill you

and anyone worth

bleeding for

would never pick up the blade.

All my favorite poetry

is about passion and intensity

maybe it's not you I love at all

but the longing to relate to my favorite art

just once I want to be able to read my favorite poem

and find a familiar face within the pages

to feel that longing

that artists create oceans for

so, you give me a teardrop

and I mistake it for a tsunami

hoping maybe for once I can relate

maybe it was never really you at all.

Your love

is holding a knife

by the blade

and

never knowing

whether or not

you left

the safety

on.

I think I know you

because I want you

but maybe I'm only hoping to close

this space in between

you'll never want

what's next to you

if your arms are always outstretched

learn to put them down.

Everytime I go back to you

I hand you the knife

maybe red was never your favorite color

maybe it's been mine all along

I'm starting to think I actually like bleeding.

To love

is not to perform

but I can't help

but do cartwheels and backflips

when you're around

in hopes you'll find me

as interesting as I deem you

so that at night

when I'm dreaming

I'm not thinking all alone

-I want to stop the act.

I reach for you

but you don't have hands

you're miles away

and I have short arms

I can write poetry but it's all in fragments

please tell me you'll still understand

Don't tell me

all this blood

was for nothing.

Maybe I'm tired

and maybe I don't love you

the nights can be long

without someone to wish for

so I close my eyes

and remember the feel

of your arms around me

though you never

really held me.

Maybe I'm lonely

so it was never really you at all

but I pretend

I'm in pain

I think sometimes I just wish I knew you

enough to miss you.

What you chase

will always run

but what if I want to find what's hiding

I know I shouldn't have to beg

but maybe my lips like pleading

One day I'll stop running

but today I can't stop

my feet from moving

One day I'll stop chasing

what simply doesn't belong to me

but today my body can't help but to invite

the pain in.

I hate you

and no I don't mean

I despise you

hate is never that simple

I hate you

because I love you

and I'm not allowed to

hate is left over seating when love has standing

room only.

If I'm a fool

for falling in love

You're a coward

for seeing it through.

I asked for a sign

and looked up

to you holding

her hand

I begged for answers

yet the clarity

is a dagger

slicing through my skin

when I asked for a sign

I didn't realize I was asking for you

and I didn't know how fast

I could lose

and how far a heart

really does drop.

I flinch

when you tell me

you love me

because I know how this ends

You drag me closer

just to slam the door

in my face

where I'll sit in the rain

for weeks

without asking

for an umbrella.

I no longer believe his favorite color is red.

I gave him every ounce of red in my being

and it still wasn't enough.

-I can't be your favorite.

I was an object

you had interest in

without rationale

you added me

to your collection

I used to have meaning.

You placed a chastity belt

around my being

I promise not to unlock

for anyone else

but at least let me hold the key.

I'm dependable in the sense that I'll always

give myself to people I know

will tear me apart.

I'm dependable at my own expense

and in favor of your selfish desires.

I know what I'm going to do

and you know what you're not.

We're dependable

in the sense we both know

you'll destroy me

and I won't stop you.

The fundamentals of irony

The greatest feeling in the world

is the worst pain in the world

once it's gone

but irony works both ways

one day you can be great again.

So what if it all matters

what if that date standing you up

is the reason you write

a young girls favorite poem

and what if those tears

you cried

were actually diamonds

what if you need to hurt

just as much as you need

to heal

and what if a heart

needs to be broken

to be put back together.

You don't notice

the grass is green

until the moment

you realize you're alive.

What is this sadness trying to teach me?

-never believe words,
believe actions

-your friends have your back
more than that boy you're crying over does
put your focus into them

-family is everything

-sometimes even if you love someone
there comes a point
when you have to let them go

-focus on those who show you
they care
not those who don't.

Perhaps getting hurt

is just as important

as being happy

the best parts

of yourself can grow

from an ache,

a longing for more

so maybe it all matters

perhaps it matters all the same.

Pour your pain

into art

and don't let

that sadness

be for nothing.

Allow yourself to be sad

about it now

but don't remain there

for too long

your life is too short

to let any individual

take it.

You pity me

for being alone,

Life is only sad

spent with those

who don't deserve you.

I cannot make you love me

and I no longer want to

I've screamed and I've shouted

but I've run out of ink

this will be the last poem

I write for you

but had you asked

I'd have written forever.

Authors Note

I want to say thank you to everyone who decided to read my first poetry book. I have been writing poetry for six years now and am so happy to finally be sharing it. The support means the world to me!

I'd also like to give a special shoutout to my parents, family, and friends. You guys are amazing and I appreciate the support throughout the years!